A rabbit is on the grass in the mist. Jelly sees it.

The rabbit runs
away. Jelly runs
after it.

The rabbit runs into a log. Jelly peeps in the log.

Jelly creeps into the log. She cannot see the rabbit.

But lots of soft fluffy
things rush past her.

Jelly comes out of
the log. She sees
seven little rabbits.

A big rabbit comes
out of the long
grass. She is cross.

She stamps her foot.
Jelly is afraid and
she runs away.